ANCIENT ROMAN ROADS AND ARCHITECTURE

CHILDREN'S ANCIENT HISTORY BOOKS

BABY PROFESSOR

EDUCATION KIDS

Speedy Publishing LLC
40 E. Main St. #1156
Newark, DE 19711
www.speedypublishing.com
Copyright 2016

Roman roads were a great factor in making travel and communications easy and hastening the work of the Romans to receive information, trade goods, and move their armies.

At the height of Rome's power, there were more than 29 military highways constructed from the city.

They cut through hills and crossed deep ravineson bridges. The road system had over 80,500 kilometer of paved roads out of a total of 400,000 kilometer of roads.

At its height, the Roman Empire had 113 provinces with 372 road links. The road builders used stones, cement mixed with broken tiles, broken stones mixed with cement and sand, and curved stones.

This allowed the water to drain so the roads won't be flooded. The top of the roads were tightly packed with paving stones.

They based the design of their roads from what was written in the Laws of the Twelve Tables which specified the width to be 8 feet and the curved part should be 16 feet.

Their ideal was to build roads that did not require frequent repairs, and they constructed them as straight as possible so they could build the narrowest road possible to save on the materials used.

The road network was very important for Rome's expansion and in maintaining the empire's stability.

When it comes to the design of their buildings, the Romans followed Greek architecture and respected its traditions, especially the Corinthian design.

Since they were great innovators, though, they used new construction materials, techniques, and combined existing techniques with creative designs so they could produce new architectural structures such as triumphal arches, basilicas, monumental aqueducts, granary buildings, amphitheaters, and residential housing blocks.

Many Rome's innovations were as a response to their changing needs. Their projects were all backed by the apparatus funded by the state and spread around the Roman world, making sure that what they built would last. In fact, many of their edifices are still present today.

Among their innovations is the Arch of Septimius Severus in Rome (CE 203). They also made columns with a composite capital that mixed the volute of the Ionic order to the acanthus leaves of Corinthian design.

The Tuscan column was used in domestic architecture. The Romans favored columns made of one huge piece of stone, compared to the Greek approach of making a column by stacking several stone segments on top of each other.

The Greek influence
on architecture was
also evident in the
Roman basilicas
and buildings
made for baths.

The Temple of Jupiter in Rome was the first building made entirely of marble materials. Carrara (Luna) was the most commonly used marble.

Aside from marble, the Romans use travertine white limestone, which they got from the quarries near Tivoli. Its inherent load-bearing strength made it useful for both for building and for precise carvings.

The Romans
were the first
to discover the
possibilities of using
lime mortar in
producing concrete.

This concrete material was cheaper than solid stones and so they used it to make more presentable façades using marble veneer, stucco, and other cheap materials such as fired brick or terracotta.

You can see that the Roman architectural designs were still followed by some people because of their elegance and durability. Yet it can be expensive compared to just using a concrete mixture.

Did you enjoy reading this book? Share this to your friends.

Visit

BABY PROFESSOR
EDUCATION KIDS

www.BabyProfessorBooks.com

to download Free Baby Professor eBooks
and view our catalog of new and exciting
Children's Books

Made in the USA
Monee, IL
15 February 2021